TRUE STORIES
FOR CHI[LDREN]

Translate[d by]

Matina Wali M[...]

Ta-Ha Publishers Ltd.

1, Wynne Road

London SW9 0BB

Re-print: 1995, 97, 99, 2001-2004 · 2006

Published by

Ta-Ha Publishers Ltd.
1 Wynne Road
London SW9 0BB

General Editor: Afsar Siddiqui
Translated by: Matina W. Muhammad
Edited by: Ahmad Thomson
Illustrated by: M. Ishaq

British Library Cataloguing in Publication Data
Muhammad, Matina Wali
True Stories for Children
I. Title

ISBN 0-907461-98-0

Typeset by Wheatley Design, Aldershot.
Printed by: Deluxe Printers, London.

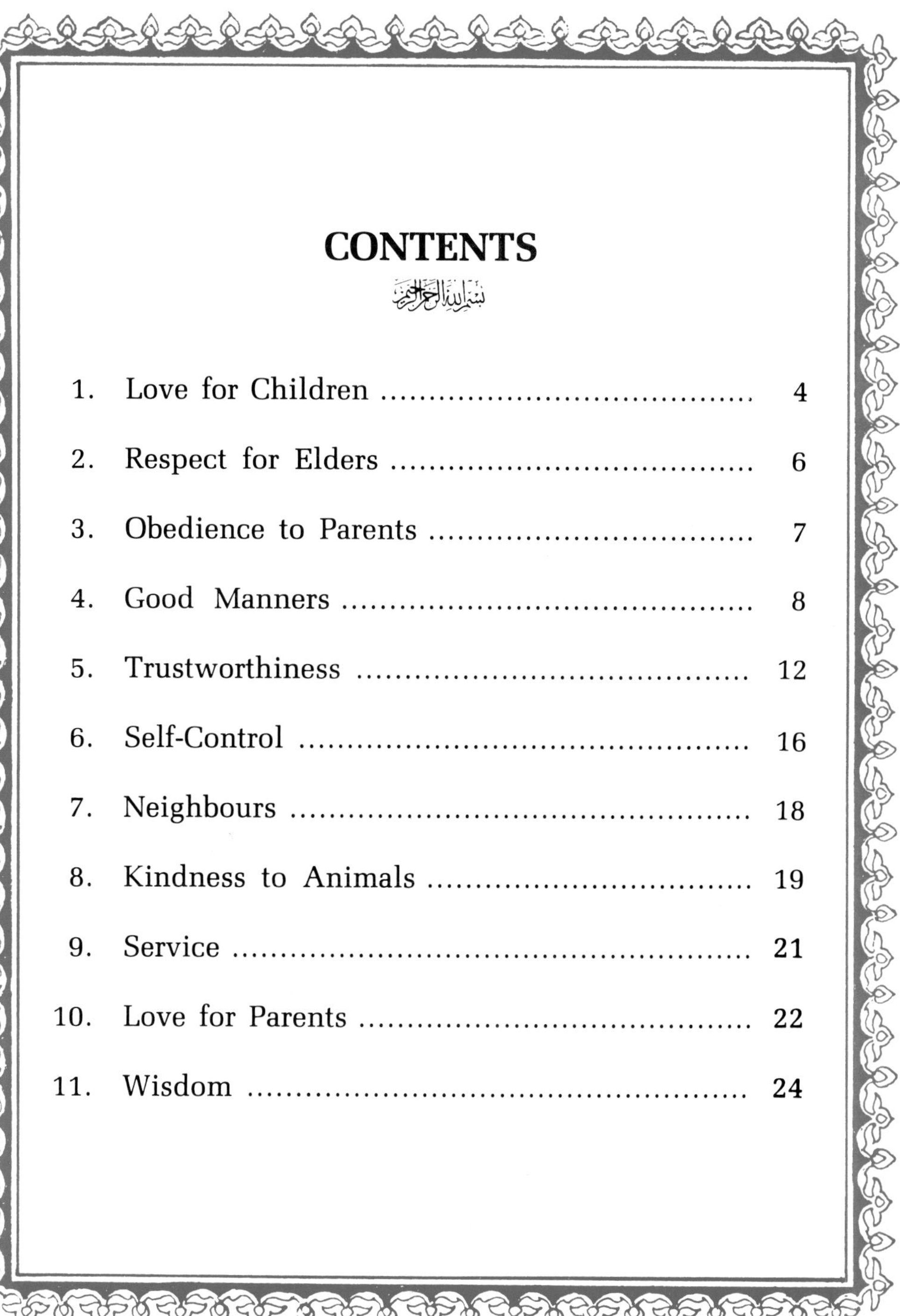

CONTENTS

1
LOVE FOR CHILDREN

A long time ago, people used to be sold as slaves in the market place just like cattle. One day, in the time of the Prophet Muhammad, may Allah bless him and grant him peace, some cruel and nasty men brought a small boy whom they had stolen from his parents to be sold in the market place in Makka. When the Prophet's wife, Khadija, came to know of this, may Allah be pleased with her, she went to the market place and bought the boy for a very small sum of money.

Khadija took the boy to the Prophet Muhammad, may the blessings and peace of Allah be on him and his family, who, because of his love for children, was saddened to see a little boy who had become separated from his parents and had no-one else to look after him.

From then on, the Prophet cared for him with such love and affection that the small boy could not even think of leaving him.

After some time had passed, the small boy's real father came to know of his son's whereabouts, and after coming to Makka his search led him to the home of the Prophet, where he was told what had happened.

On hearing that Khadija had bought his son for a very small sum of money, he tried to buy him back for the same amount, but the Prophet would not permit this. Instead he gave the boy his freedom, saying that he should be where he wanted to be.

The small boy, however, had grown so close to the Prophet Muhammad and Khadija after living with them in love and harmony that he had no desire to leave them. He clung to the Prophet's legs and begged his father to leave him where he was.

The kind father smiled lovingly and agreed to let him stay with the Prophet Muhammad and Khadija, may Allah bless them and grant them peace, knowing that his son was in better hands, far better than he could ever provide.

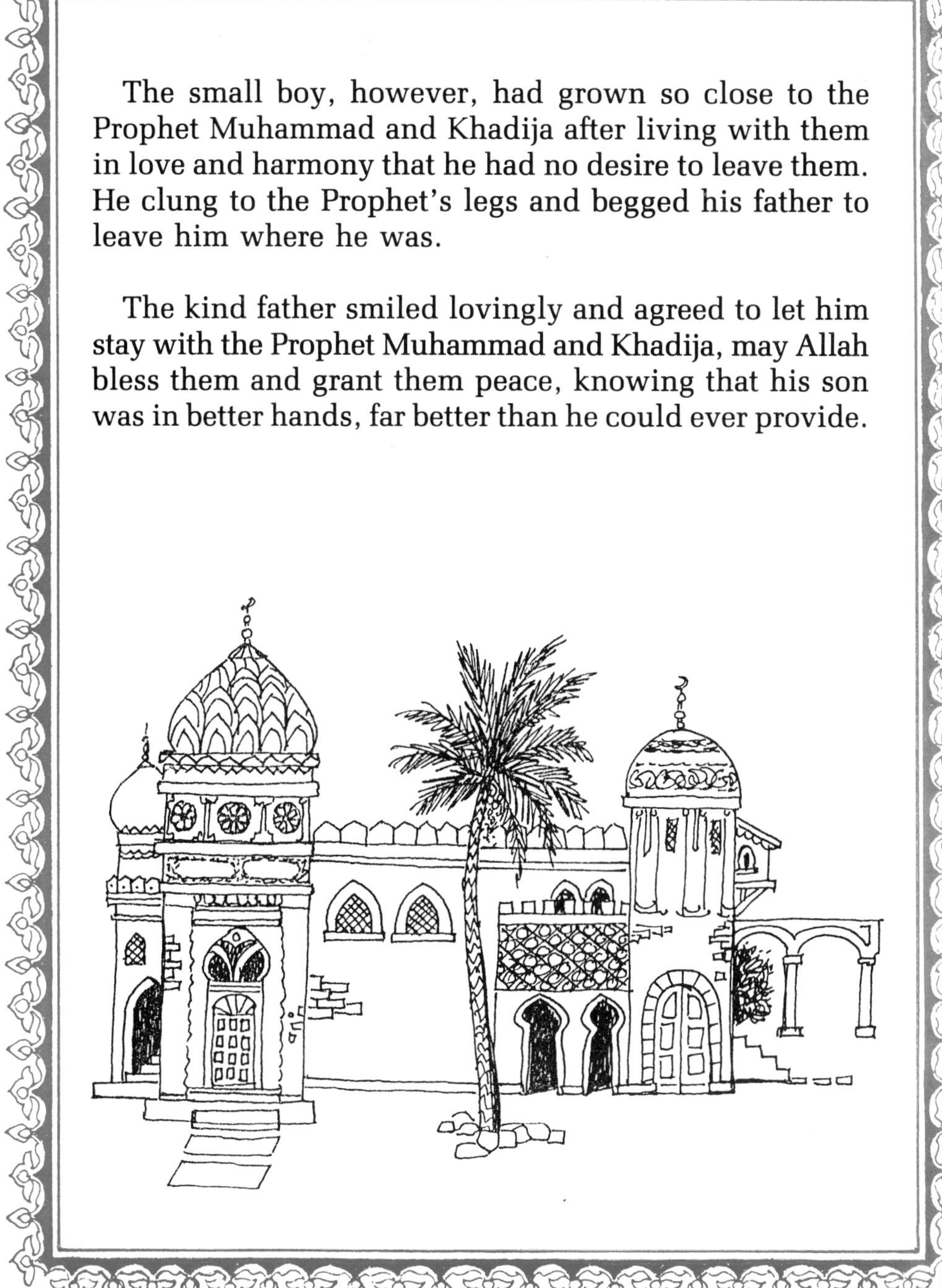

2
RESPECT FOR ELDERS

One day *sayyedina* Abu Bakr and *sayyedina* Umar, together with Umar's son, Abdullah, were sitting with the Prophet Muhammad, may the blessings and peace of Allah be on him and his family and his companions. The Prophet asked them a question: "Which tree most resembles the Muslims in its excellence, gives fruit each year and is not affected even by the autumn?"

Neither of his two companions knew the answer, but Abdullah, the son of Umar, knew it immediately — it was the date palm of course. He wanted to say it out loud, but because both his father and Abu Bakr remained silent, he did not want to speak out of turn. He too remained silent.

Later on, when *sayyedina* Umar came to know that Abdullah had known the answer all along, he asked him why he had kept quiet:

"If you knew the answer," he said, "why didn't you say so? I would have been very proud to see you answer a riddle that no-one else could."

"How could I speak out when you and Abu Bakr remained silent?" replied Abdullah. "It would have been a sign of disrespect towards you both, for you are my elders."

Sayyedina Umar was very pleased at his son's reply.

3
OBEDIENCE TO PARENTS

It is well known that the Prophet Muhammad, may the blessings and peace of Allah be on him, would never accept a charitable gift, either for himself or for his family. He would always give such gifts to someone else, especially to the poor and to those who were in need.

On one occasion some people offered some dates to the Prophet as a charitable gift. He reminded them that he could not accept them for himself or his family, and put them on a window ledge in order to distribute them later on.

At that time *sayyedina* Hussayn, one of the Prophet's grandsons, was still a small boy, and when he passed by the window, he saw the dates just waiting to be eaten. He did not know that these dates were a charitable gift for the poor, so he reached up to the window-ledge, picked a date and put it in his mouth!

As it happened, the Prophet Muhammad saw what Hussayn had done and asked him to spit it out:

"Hussayn!" he said. "Take that date out of your mouth and throw it away, because it is *sadaqa*, and I and my family are not permitted to accept or eat anything intended as *sadaqa*."

Sayyedina Hussayn immediately took the date out of his mouth and threw it away.

4
GOOD MANNERS

One day, when *sayyedina* Hassan and *sayyedina* Hussain, were still small boys, an old *bedouin* from the desert visited their home in Madina. The old man was new to Islam and still ignorant. When it was time to do the prayer and the old man began to do *wudu*, it soon became apparent that he did not know how to do *wudu* properly.

Hassan and Hussain both knew that it is necessary to do *wudu* correctly and wanted to show the old *bedouin* how to do it, but at first they were not sure how to tell him. If he were to be told plainly by two small boys that he did not even know how to do *wudu*, he might feel awkward or embarrassed.

Fortunately they thought of a good way to teach him without having to openly point out his mistakes. After putting some water in a jug, they too prepared to do *wudu*, but before starting they asked the old *bedouin* to watch them:

"Excuse us, old man," they said respectfully, "we want to make sure that we are doing *wudu* properly: please would you watch us and tell us if we make any mistakes."

Having said this, they both did *wudu* exactly as it should be done, with the old *bedouin* intently watching them.

By the time they had both finished, he had learned how to do *wudu* correctly without having been made to feel at all embarrassed.

"Yes." he said with a smile, "you both know how to do *wudu* perfectly!"

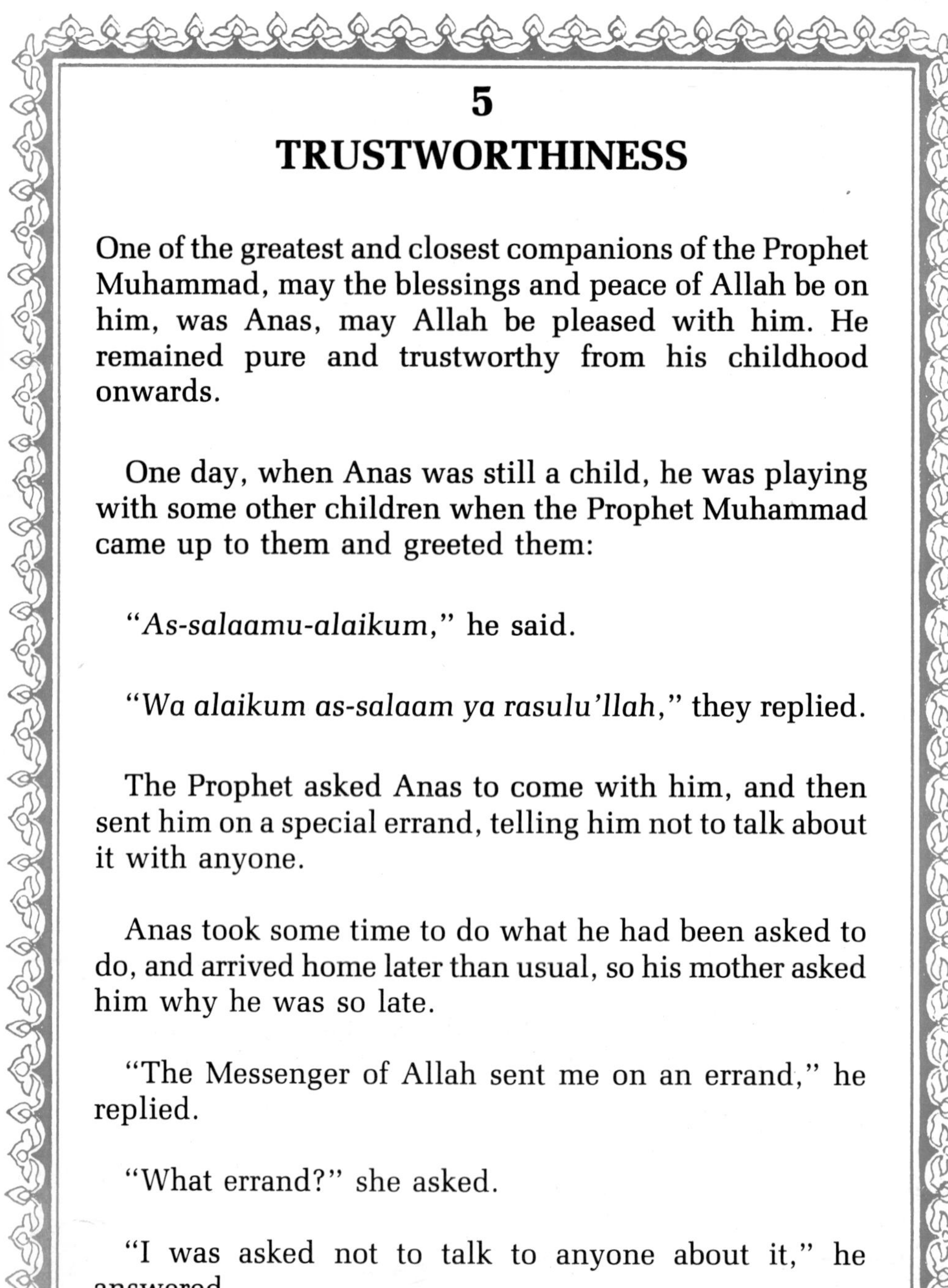

5
TRUSTWORTHINESS

One of the greatest and closest companions of the Prophet Muhammad, may the blessings and peace of Allah be on him, was Anas, may Allah be pleased with him. He remained pure and trustworthy from his childhood onwards.

One day, when Anas was still a child, he was playing with some other children when the Prophet Muhammad came up to them and greeted them:

"*As-salaamu-alaikum,*" he said.

"*Wa alaikum as-salaam ya rasulu'llah,*" they replied.

The Prophet asked Anas to come with him, and then sent him on a special errand, telling him not to talk about it with anyone.

Anas took some time to do what he had been asked to do, and arrived home later than usual, so his mother asked him why he was so late.

"The Messenger of Allah sent me on an errand," he replied.

"What errand?" she asked.

"I was asked not to talk to anyone about it," he answered.

"Then it is a secret," she said, "so do not tell this secret to anyone."

Anas remembered his mother's words for as long as he lived, and he never told the secret to anyone, even to his closest friend, who was called Thabit:

"Thabit," he said, when telling him about this incident one day, "if I were to ever tell this secret to anyone, it would be to you, but I will do as I have been asked for as long as I live."

6
SELF-CONTROL

During a battle in the way of Allah, *sayyedina* Ali, found himself face to face with a *kafir* who attacked him violently. They were both brave and powerful men, but the *kafir* was no match for *sayyedina* Ali, who was soon sitting astride his chest, ready to finish him off.

"I invite you to bear witness that there is no god except Allah, and that Muhammad is the Messenger of Allah," said Ali. "Accept Islam, and your life will be spared."

"Never!" panted the *kafir*.

Sayyedina Ali lifted his sword and was just about to plunge it into his enemy, when the *kafir* spat defiantly in his face.

Much to the *kafir's* surprise, *sayyedina* Ali immediately jumped away from his enemy and lowered his sword.

"Go away!" said *sayyedina* Ali, "I cannot kill you now."

"Why did you do that?" asked the *kafir*. "You could have killed me easily."

"I was fighting you purely in the way of Allah," replied Ali, "but when you spat in my face, your insult made me angry and if I had killed you in anger, it would have taken me to the Fire — so I had no choice but to let you

go. To kill someone in anger or out of a desire for revenge is not bravery, but the act of a coward."

On hearing this, the *kafir* was so impressed by *sayyedina* Ali's sincerity and self-control that he embraced Islam on the spot:

"I bear witness that there is no god except Allah," he said, "and I bear witness that Muhammad is the Messenger of Allah."

7
NEIGHBOURS

The people who always kept the company of the Prophet Muhammad, may Allah bless him and grant him peace, were the best of people, and they always treated others with great consideration and generosity.

One of the Prophet's companions was called Abdullah. He feared Allah and was kind to people. One of his neighbours was a Jew.

One morning Abdullah sacrificed a goat for his family to eat that evening, and then left his house to go about his business for the day.

When Abdullah returned to his house that night, the evening meal was placed before him. He and his family were just about to start eating, when Abdullah asked his family if they had given some of the meat to their neighbours. They replied that they had not given any to the Jew because he was not a Muslim.

"What!" said Abdullah. "He may be a Jew, but he is still our neighbour. The Messenger of Allah, may Allah bless him and grant him peace, has often reminded us to be kind towards our neighbours, even if they are not Muslims. I will not eat anything until he has been given some of this meat!"

It was not very long before Abdullah and his family were enjoying their evening meal!

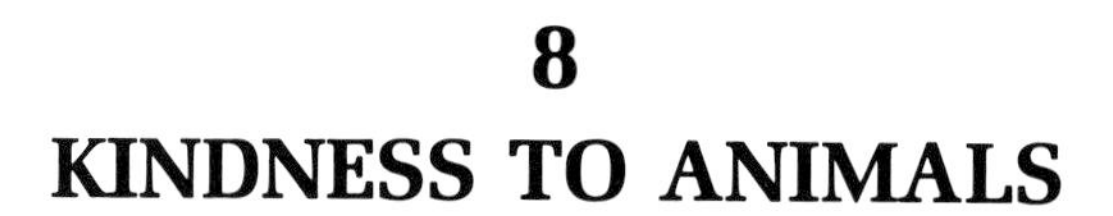

8
KINDNESS TO ANIMALS

One day one of the companions of the Prophet Muhammad, may Allah bless him and grant him peace, was walking down a path when he heard the sound of cheeping coming from a nearby bush. He went over to have a closer look and discovered a large nest with several small baby birds inside. They had not yet learnt to fly and were anxiously calling on their mother who had flown off to find them some food.

Without really thinking about what he was doing, the man picked them up one by one and wrapped them loosely in a piece of cloth. Just as he was leaving to continue on his way, the mother returned to the nest with food for her babies in her beak, only to find it empty.

She could hear her children cheeping frantically for her from inside the cloth, and in her agitation she flew over the man's head several times, calling out to her chicks in desperation, but the man did not appear to notice her and walked on down the path until he eventually joined the Prophet Muhammad, may Allah bless him and grant him peace.

When the Prophet heard the small birds' muffled cheeping coming from inside the man's bundle, he asked him where they had come from. When he had heard the man's story, the Prophet, who was a very kind and compassionate man, pointed out that the man's actions had caused distress both to the young birds and to their mother

alike, and asked him to return the chicks immediately to where they belonged — in the nest, in the bush, with their mother!

9
SERVICE

There have been many rightly-guided *khalifs* in the past whose qualities were far more refined and noble than those of today's kings, prime ministers and presidents. They lived very simply and spent very little on their own personal comfort. One of these great *khalifs* was called Umar ibn Abdal-Aziz. He followed the teachings of Islam with sincerity and served the people whom he ruled with humility.

One hot summer's night Umar ibn Abdal-Aziz was lying awake in bed, too hot to sleep, but cooled a little at least by the fan with which a maidservant was fanning him. Thanks to her efforts he at last fell asleep. After a while, however, she began to grow very tired and then finally she too fell asleep, the fan slipping from her fingers and falling to the floor.

The *khalif* awoke from his slumber, and seeing that his maidservant had fallen asleep, he picked up the fan and began to fan her gently. After a while she woke up and was startled and dismayed to find the *khalif* fanning her. She was meant to be fanning him — what would happen to her now?

"Do not worry." said Umar ibn Abdal-Aziz with a smile, "you are just as much a human being as I am. When I needed to sleep, you kept me cool, and when you needed sleep I kept you cool. What's wrong with that?"

10
LOVE FOR PARENTS

A long time ago there was a young boy who loved his mother very much. His name was Sharafud-Din and he was destined to grow up to become a very good, kind and considerate saint.

Once, when Sharafud-Din was still small, his mother fell very ill and had to stay in bed. One night she awoke with a burning thirst and called out to her son to bring her a bowl of water.

The young boy hurried to do her bidding, but when he returned to her bedside with the water, he discovered that she had fallen asleep again. Sharafud-Din was not sure what to do. Should he wake her up, or wait until she awoke, or leave the water by her bedside and go back to bed himself? He decided to wait until she awoke.

Minutes passed ... hours passed ... the night passed ... and still the small boy waited patiently with the water at his mother's side. Finally his mother awoke a little after the first light of dawn had paled the sky, and to her surprise there was her beloved son at her side.

"How long have you been standing here?" she asked. "You haven't been there all night have you?"

'Yes, mother," he replied, "I have been here since you asked me to bring you some water."

His mother was deeply touched by his devotion, and asked Allah to pour His blessings on her son. One day he would become a very great saint!

11
WISDOM

A long time ago, there was a very famous *khalif* in Baghdad who was called Harun ar-Rashid. He had two sons, called Ameen and Mamun, who used to be taught by a wise old man who would sit with them cross-legged on the floor.

One day Ameen and Mamun had just finished their morning's lessons, and when their teacher rose to his feet, they both ran to fetch his slippers for him, before he had even taken a step.

The two boys reached their teacher's slippers at exactly the same time, and in the same moment they both grabbed hold of them, each wanting to be the one who placed them ready for their teacher to step into them.

The teacher soon settled their quarrel — before they had a chance to tear his slippers apart!

"One of you put one slipper ready, and the other one of you put the other slipper ready," he said with a smile, and in this way they both helped him with his slippers.

When Harun ar-Rashid heard about what had happened, he was very amused and gave each of them a reward, and when Ameen and Mamun grew to manhood, each became a ruler.

What do you think the wise old teacher would have said if there had been *three* sons?